Power

and

Grace

— A Guide to the —
Catholic Sacraments

ASCENSION

West Chester, Pennsylvania

Ascension
Post Office Box 1990
West Chester, PA 19380
1-800-376-0520
ascensionpress.com

Printed in the United States of America

ISBN 978-1-945179-64-8

CONTENTS

INTRODUCTION

As a Catholic, you have encountered the sacraments throughout your life. Though you probably have little memory of your Baptism, this was your first sacramental experience. Then, as a grade schooler, you were introduced to Reconciliation (or First Penance, as it was called "back in the day") and the Eucharist. A little while later, you received a strengthening of the Holy Spirit at Confirmation. If you ever suffered an injury or serious illness, you may have been blessed to receive the Anointing of the Sick. If you are married, at your wedding you formed a union with your spouse that images the union of Christ and his Bride, the Church.

Have you ever wondered why the sacraments are so important to our Catholic Faith? Have you every desired a deeper understanding of these "mysteries" of the Faith? This program, *Power and Grace,* seeks to present the power of the sacraments as the means to a life of grace in the Holy Spirit.

This short book is designed to accompany the video portion of *Power and Grace* and to serve as a "stand-alone" resource presenting the "nuts and bolts" of the seven sacraments. (*Note:* The video presentations of this program have been adapted from the popular Ascension faith formation resources *Chosen, Altaration, Belonging,*

YOU, and *God's Plan for a Joy-Filled Marriage*.) The book is divided into four parts, and the content of its chapters expands upon the insights presented in the video segments. The video segment that corresponds to each chapter is listed below (in brackets):

Part I – The Power and Purpose of the Sacraments

Chapter 1: The Gift of Grace
[Session 1, Segment 1 – Nashville Dominicans, *Chosen*]

Chapter 2: Sacraments and Grace
[Session 1, Segment 2 – Nashville Dominicans, *Chosen*]

Chapter 3: Sacraments in Your Life –What If?
[Session 1, Segment 3 – Mark Hart, *Altaration*]

Part II – Chosen by God

Chapter 4: The Sacraments of Initiation
[Session 2, Segment 1 – Nashville Dominicans, *Chosen*]

Chapter 5: Baptism
[Session 2, Segment 2 – Fr. Mike Schmitz, *Belonging*]

Chapter 6: Confirmation
[Session 2, Segment 3 – Chris Stefanick, *Chosen*]

Chapter 7: Eucharist
[Session 2, Segment 4 – Fr. Mike Schmitz, *Altaration*]

Part III – Finding God

Chapter 8: The Sacraments of Healing
[Session 3, Segment 1 – Nashville Dominicans, *Chosen*]

Chapter 9: Reconciliation
[Session 3, Segment 2 – Fr. Mike Schmitz, *Chosen*]

Chapter 10: Anointing of the Sick
[Session 3, Segment 3 – Fr. Mark Toups, *Chosen*]

Part IV – Service for God

Chapter 11: The Sacraments of Service
[Session 4, Segment 1 – Nashville Dominicans, *Chosen*]

Chapter 12: Holy Orders
[Session 4, Segment 2 – Fr. Josh Johnson/Brian Butler, *YOU*]

Chapter 13: Matrimony
[Session 4, Segment 3 – Older Couple, *God's Plan*]

Chapter 14: Living the Seven Sacraments
[Session 4, Segment 4 – Nashville Dominicans, *Chosen*]

As you can see, each "Part" of this book corresponds to a "Session" of the *Power and Grace* video presentations, and each "Chapter" is related to a particular video segment. For example, this program could be conducted over a four-week period, with one session per week. The various segments of a particular session would be shown during a single meeting. (As each segment is brief, sixty to ninety minutes would be sufficient to show all of the segments, including time for discussion.)

Discussion questions are included at the end of each chapter. These questions are intended to spark discussion after viewing each video segment or reading each chapter. The related book content complements the video presentations, and groups can decide to read this written content either before or after each group session. (More information on how to run a *Power and Grace* small-group program is available at ascensionpress.com.)

It is our sincere hope that your appreciation of—and love for—these wonderful mysteries of our Faith will increase abundantly through *Power and Grace*.

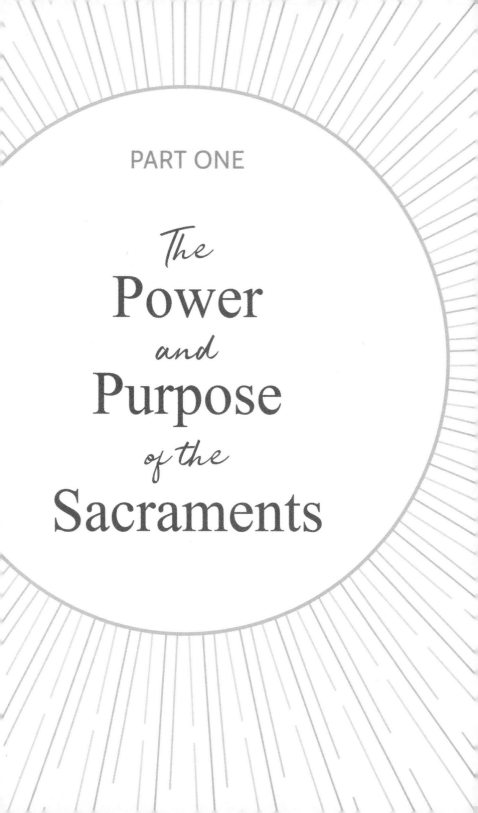

PART ONE

The
Power
and
Purpose
of the
Sacraments

See my children; the treasure of a Christian is not on the earth, it is in heaven. Well, our thoughts ought to be where our treasure is.

St. John Vianney

Chapter One

THE GIFT OF GRACE

What do you seek?

What have you been made for? What would satisfy you deep in the core of your being? Some days, a power nap or a really good snack might seem to be enough. During our more ambitious moments, we may yearn for something bigger, maybe success or even greatness. But the most enjoyable pleasures—a project well done or winning a championship—all eventually fade and open up another quest for *more*.

On the one hand, we are too easily satisfied, while on the other, we are insatiable. We tend to settle for little bits of satisfaction that are just enough to keep us at ease the way we are. Yet, we always hunger for more. Many have noted this persistent aspect of the human condition, but the question remains: "What have we been made for?" Isn't it more than the status quo? Isn't it more than what we are focusing our energy on this week? Why are we restless, longing for more?

How frequently do we think, *"If only ..." If only I had a different house, a different job, a different spouse. If only I had more money or recognition. If only I were better looking. If only I had more friends.* The list goes on ... While any one of these factors might give us a piece of satisfaction, all human persons—even those who are rich, famous, and beautiful—are restless and longing and aching because we have been created for something this world simply cannot offer. We have been made for heaven.

In the Gospel of John, Jesus dispensed with small talk when he called the first apostles. There were no icebreakers, no cocktail party introductions, no "Hi, I'm Jesus and I enjoy long walks in the desert. What's your favorite book of the Torah?" Instead, he went right to the heart, asking, "What do you seek?" (John 1:38). In response, these two disciples left everything behind to follow Jesus. Why? Because they perceived in Jesus the answer to what they truly sought—God himself, in the flesh, the One through whom all things exist, the Living Bread come down from heaven, the Living Water, the Good Shepherd, the Way, the Truth, and the Life. Like each of us, they were made for him and destined to be with him in heaven forever.

> # Everything
> ## is a *grace!*
>
> St. Thérèse of Lisieux

All is grace

Those in religious vocations—priests, religious brothers, and religious sisters—are a particularly startling and hopeful sign of our destiny. Men and women who voluntarily and joyfully embrace poverty, celibacy, and obedience, with their counter-cultural witness, radiate hope to the world. This is why we remain in awe of St. Teresa of Calcutta (Mother Teresa) and why we talk about St. Francis of Assisi and place statues of him in our gardens almost eight centuries after his death. These religious men and women forsake the goods of pleasure, materials, success, and even the good of marriage in favor of beginning heaven now. What have they found that makes this sacrifice worthwhile? What is their secret to joy? They will tell you: *grace*. St. Thérèse of Lisieux, one of history's most popular saints, summed up the whole mystery of her life—which was quite ordinary, yet captivated millions—very simply: "Everything is a grace."

Grace is the free gift of God's life within our souls. Take time to ponder this amazing truth—*the free gift of God's life within us*. This is a bold claim. First, grace isn't something we earn. God does not give us his life because we go to church, because we are pious enough, or because we choose a religious vocation. Grace is not a prize; it is a free, unconditional gift of God's love. Second, the grace God gives us is a participation in his own divine life. He makes us sharers in his own divine nature (see 2 Peter 1:4). This divine sharing means many amazing things, not the least of which is eternal life! Grace means that we are God's children (see 1 John 3:1) and that, ultimately, we will be made like God and see him as he is (see 1 John 3:2).

Grace and happiness

God's life within us is the only source of fulfillment and happiness that thoroughly satisfies the human heart. Why? Because the very purpose of our existence, God's very reason for making us, is unconditional love. He made us to love us, to share his life with us (see CCC 1). Our creation by divine love and our design for

> Few souls understand what God would accomplish in them if they were to abandon themselves unreservedly to him and if they were to allow his grace to mold them accordingly.
>
> *St. Ignatius of Loyola*

divine life are gifts. God desired to bestow these gifts even before we existed. When our first parents sinned and rejected his gifts, he restored humanity to himself through the Passion, death, and resurrection of Jesus. This restoration is through grace.

So how does grace operate? Does grace merely cover over and conceal our brokenness? Does grace erase our personalities and make us into "holy robots"? No! We must actively choose to receive the gift of grace, following the perfect example set by Mary at the Annunciation. Like Mary, when God invites, offers, and calls us, we can respond, *"Fiat!* Yes!"* When we do this, we open ourselves to being freer and happier than we could ever imagine. While God's grace does not exempt us from difficulties and suffering in this life, it does offer us peace and gives our suffering meaning. Grace builds upon nature. Grace refines us to become our truest selves and empowers us to become holier. Grace prepares us for heaven.

Grace is nothing else than a beginning of *glory* in us.

St. Thomas Aquinas

DISCUSSION QUESTIONS

1. Reflecting on his own dissatisfaction with passing things, St. Augustine famously said, referring to God, "Our hearts are restless ... until they rest in you." How do you experience this restlessness? What do you cling to despite finding that it fails to satisfy? Have you ever had a taste of the "rest" that comes from God?

2. Describe grace in your own words. How have you experienced grace as a free and unearned gift in your life?

3. Who makes grace credible to you? Is there a person you have encountered who seems to be "full of grace"? What makes you think so?

> *Grace* builds on nature.
>
> — *St. Thomas Aquinas*

> *Oh,* how senseless we are! The good God calls us to him, and we fly from him! He wishes to make us happy, and we will not have his happiness. He commands us to love him, and we give our hearts to the devil. We employ in ruining ourselves the time he gives us to save our souls. We make war upon him with the means he gave us to serve him.
>
> — *St. John Vianney*

Tips

- Combined with prayer, fasting is a powerful and effective way to reorient our hearts and minds toward heaven. While fasting is usually refraining from food, it can also be sacrificing other comforts or pleasurable activities for a certain period of time. Work on developing a habit of fasting. Start with something simple such as drinking your coffee without cream, turning off the radio in your car, or abstaining from social media for a day.

- Journal your answer to Jesus' opening question in John's Gospel: "What do you seek?"

- Read the lives of saints, who are witnesses to the power of grace. While we are not necessarily called to imitate a particular saint in every detail, we can be encouraged by—and seek to imitate—their close relationship with God. When we do that, we become the person God made us to be.

- Strive to be more aware of grace working in your life. When you pass a church, for example, say a brief prayer of gratitude or reflect briefly on the Real Presence of Jesus in the Eucharist. Pray like the father who brought his child to be healed by Jesus: "I believe; help my unbelief!" (Mark 9:24).

Every true prayer is a prayer of the Church; by means of that prayer the Church prays, since it is the Holy Spirit living in the Church.

St. Edith Stein

Chapter Two
WHAT IS A SACRAMENT?

More Than a Milestone

The word "sacrament" is familiar to nearly every Catholic. Most know that there are seven sacraments, and many Catholics see sacraments as important rites of passage that mark life's milestones, such as Baptism, Confirmation, and Marriage. Yet the sacraments are much richer than merely rites of passage or family customs. They are true encounters with Jesus Christ.

Here are some essential points about the sacraments.

Sacraments are efficacious signs

What exactly is an "efficacious sign"? "Efficacious" means that something works, that it is "effective." Naturally, we all like it when things work and are not too pleased when they don't. In theological terms, a "sign" is a visible representation of an invisible reality. So an *efficacious sign* makes the thing it signifies happen. Signs point toward things that we cannot see, but sacraments do more than just point—they actually make incredible things happen. More specifically, sacraments make grace happen (see CCC 1131).

Think about the app icons on your smartphone. They are visible representations of the music or the messages that exist on the device. These icons are "efficacious"— when you tap one, it makes the app appear. Similarly, sacraments do more than merely *symbolize* grace; they actually make grace present and confer it to us. Here is a central, beautiful, and mysterious Catholic teaching. The sacraments actually do what they claim to do; they are far more than symbols or milestones. As we look at each sacrament in this study, this richness will become clearer.

When we really ponder the sacraments, they can seem somewhat strange. The pouring of water over the head and the words of baptism free us from original sin and bring us into communion with the Church? In the Mass, ordinary bread and wine, when consecrated by a priest, become the Body and Blood of Jesus? Whose idea was all of this? Actually, it was Jesus' idea.

Christ instituted the sacraments

All seven sacraments can be found in Scripture because they were instituted by Christ himself. Let's take a quick look:

1. *Baptism:* Before ascending into heaven forty days after Easter, Jesus commissions the disciples to baptize "in the name of the Father and of the Son and of the Holy Spirit" (see Matthew 28:19-20).

2. *Holy Eucharist:* Jesus specifically commands his apostles to eat his flesh and drink his blood (see John 6). At the Last Supper, he gives them the ability to do that (see Luke 22:19).

3. *Confirmation:* Jesus "breathed" on the apostles, saying, "Receive the Holy Spirit" (John 20:22). The Holy Spirit came as a driving wind and tongues of flame over their heads, empowering them to reach full maturity in their faith (see Acts 2).

4. *Reconciliation:* Jesus instituted the sacrament of Reconciliation with these words to his apostles: "'Peace be with you. As the

Father has sent me, even so I send you.' And when he had said this, he breathed on them, and said to them, 'Receive the Holy Spirit. If you forgive the sins of any, they are forgiven; if you retain the sins of any, they are retained'" (John 20:22-23).

5. *Anointing of the Sick:* Jesus healed and appointed his apostles to continue anointing those who were ill (see Mark 6:13; James 5:14-15).

6. *Matrimony:* Jesus restores marriage to its original dignity by becoming the Bridegroom of his Bride, the Church. Christian marriage is a public sign of Christ and the Church (see Matthew 19:8, Ephesians 5:22-33).

7. *Holy Orders:* Jesus, at the Last Supper, instituted the priesthood by calling on the apostles to celebrate the Eucharist: "Do this in remembrance of me" (Luke 22:19).

In these accounts and others, Jesus gives us the sacraments not as afterthoughts but as the central legacy that continues after his ascension into heaven. During his three years of public ministry, Jesus acted in a way that was thoroughly sacramental, continually working through efficacious signs. He formed his apostles to do likewise. In the letters

> The sacramental signs consist in sensible things: just as in the Divine Scriptures spiritual things are set before us under the guise of things sensible.
>
> *St. Thomas Aquinas*

of Paul (see 1 Corinthians 11) and James (see James 5), as well as throughout the Acts of the Apostles, we see that the sacraments formed the heart of the early Church.

The sacraments have been entrusted to the Church

Why did Jesus establish a Church, as we see him discuss with Peter (see Matthew 16:18)? Why did Jesus ascend to heaven, instead of staying with his disciples? Why did Jesus say to them, "It is to your advantage that I go" (John 16:7)? As Jesus' life moved from Cross to Resurrection to Ascension, his mission was accomplished. The bittersweet moment of the Ascension paved the way for the coming of the Spirit at Pentecost, which began the mission of the Church to preach the Gospel and minister throughout the entire world. By establishing the sacraments and a Church to perpetuate them, Jesus remained truly present in the world. As St. Leo the Great put it, "Jesus has passed over into his mysteries [sacraments]."

> *Sacraments* "effect what they signify."
>
> St. Thomas Aquinas

While the sacraments have been entrusted to those who administer them (bishops, priests, and deacons), they have also been entrusted to all who receive them, because grace makes us sharers in God's own life. Were you baptized? Then Christ has entered into your very soul; he lives in the world through you. Do you receive the Eucharist? Then Jesus lives and moves in you as his tabernacle. Have you been confirmed? Then Jesus' mission continues in you through the power of the Holy Spirit. Jesus chose us, the Church, to be his presence in the world.

The sacraments transmit divine life

As we have seen, sacraments are efficacious signs that were entrusted to the Church by Jesus himself to transmit grace, to give us a share in divine life. Communicating grace, then, is the core mission of the Church. We live and move so that the free gift of God's life can be spread throughout the world. Grace is a gift that we are called to receive through the Eucharist and Reconciliation. Grace is a gift that transformed the very core of your being at Baptism and a gift that you were called to share with the world at Confirmation. God's life is in the world through you, particularly through your participation in the sacraments as the source of grace. Through this sharing in divine life, we become more "like God," and to the extent that we share in God's own life, we make him more present in the world.

Here is an example of how sacramental grace has everyday implications. Every Sunday at Mass, we encounter Jesus truly present in the Holy Eucharist. The English word *mass* is from the Latin *missa*, meaning "sent." Thus, the sacrament received at Mass fills us with transformative grace and *sends* us into our families, our jobs, our circles of friends so that we can carry this grace in our everyday activities. The divine life we receive in the sacraments is the fuel for doing the ordinary in an extraordinary way, for blazing a trail toward heaven in all that we do.

DISCUSSION QUESTIONS

1. How can we be better witnesses to others that
    the sacraments are efficacious signs rather than
    simply milestones or rites of passage? What has
    helped or hindered you from understanding this
    in your own life?

2. How have you encountered Jesus in the
    sacraments? What can you do to encounter Jesus
    more deeply?

3. Why does it matter that Christ instituted
    the sacraments?

4. As a member of the Church, how can you take
    up the sacramental mission of transmitting or
    communicating grace in your daily life?

Tips

- *Sacramentals* remind us of God's grace and prepare our minds and hearts to receive the sacraments (see CCC 1667). Crucifixes, rosaries, medals, statues, icons, and blessings are some examples. By incorporating sacramentals into your daily routine, you will be better disposed to celebrate the sacraments.

- Make a thorough confession as part of this study of the sacraments. Various examinations of conscience can be found online to help you prepare.

What was visible in our Savior has passed over into his *mysteries*.

St. Leo the Great

One life is all we have and we live it as we believe in living it. But to sacrifice what you are and to live without belief, that is a fate more terrible than dying.

St. Joan of Arc

Chapter Three

SACRAMENTS IN YOUR LIFE

The transforming power of the sacraments

Take a moment to ponder what the Church teaches about the sacraments. What if it is all true? How could this transform your life?

What if bread and wine really become the Body and Blood of Christ during Mass? What if we truly receive the Body, Blood, soul, and divinity of Jesus in the Eucharist? What if Baptism really and irrevocably transforms each of us into a child of God? What if our sins really are forgiven in the sacrament of Reconciliation? What if we really are made new by God's grace?

If all of this is true, then there are some serious—and wonderful—implications. The happiness we seek is found in God, the God who is found in his sacraments. Faith is required to integrate this radical truth in our lives. We can *say* we believe in the power of the sacraments, but we need to believe it firmly and live it in our lives.

True belief can challenge us. We can think of the father who brought his child to Jesus, desperate for a healing miracle, and cried out simultaneously both "I believe!" and "Help my unbelief!" (Mark 9:24). As we turn more intentionally to Jesus, our faith becomes more and more integrated with our minds, hearts, thoughts, and decisions. This happens over time, often gradually; authentic faith is not a feeling that surges and fades. Faith is a gift from God that moves in our will and our choices and cooperates with our intellect. Faith compels us to seek, sincerely and openly, the answer to the question: "What if all this is true?"

The Church challenges us to see beyond the physical and visible. With our senses we perceive only bread, wine, oil, and water. We need to probe more deeply, challenge our senses, and look with the eyes of faith. Grace is both revealed and hidden in the sacraments—the visible, sensory elements reveal the sacraments, but the invisible reality of grace is "hidden" within them. For example, if we find Mass boring, we need to see beyond the visible to the reality of what is really happening and engage with more than our eyes and ears.

> You cannot be half a saint; you must be a whole saint or no saint *at all.*
>
> St. Thérèse of Lisieux

If our faith practice becomes too comfortable, too routine, we could begin to take the claims of Jesus and the Church for granted. We can go through the motions of sacramental life and miss what they really communicate. Such complacence can happen even to very devout people. Asking *"What if?"* often can keep us from apathy or boredom.

The answer will boggle our minds! If Jesus actually is who he says he is, the Church actually is what it says it is, and the sacraments do actually convey the grace they signify through physical signs, then the world is a much more beautiful place and our destiny is eternal.

DISCUSSION QUESTIONS

1. Take some time in silent prayer, and reflect on the question, "What if the sacraments are what they claim to be?" Discuss your thoughts with the group.

2. How should believing in the power of the sacraments affect the way we enter into the Mass?

3. Talk about your own experience of belief and doubt when it comes to the power of the sacraments.

"

How many of you say: I should like to see his face, his garments, his shoes. You do see him, you touch him, you eat him. He gives himself to you, not only that you may see him, but also to be your food and nourishment.

- St. John Chrysostom

"

Tip

- Go to a Eucharistic adoration chapel and reflect on the question: "What if I am face to face with the living God, right now?"

What our *senses* fail to fathom, let us grasp through faith's consent.

St. Thomas Aquinas

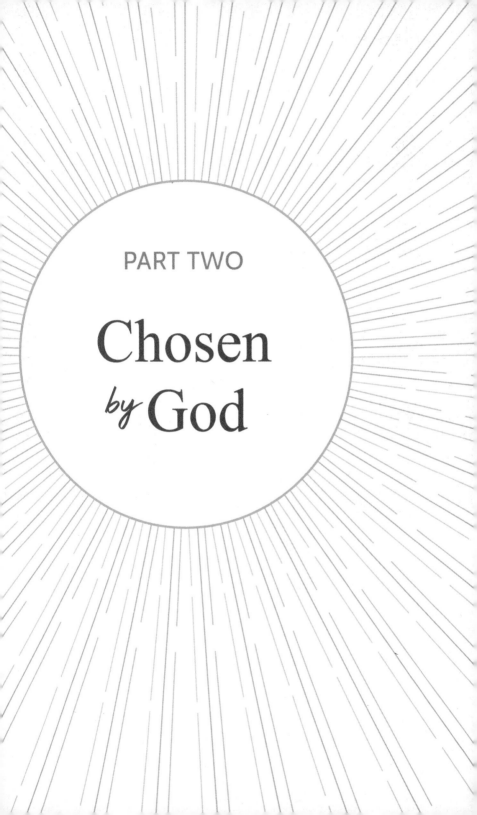

PART TWO

Chosen *by* God

He cannot have
God for his Father
who does not
have the Church
for his mother.

St. Cyprian of Carthage

Chapter Four

SACRAMENTS OF INITIATION

Made to belong

Initiation: to be brought into a group from the outside. Most of us
have experienced initiation into teams, clubs, or organizations of
some kind. When we first join a group, there are things we need
to learn and understand. There is a history, a mission, a shared
vision. Through initiation, we find ourselves bonded to other group
members and are brought into a shared purpose and set of values.
We celebrate together, support one another through difficulties, and
strive toward a common mission. Being part of something bigger
than ourselves can be a fulfilling experience, and we can find deep
meaning through belonging.

This belonging is something we desire. Think about the heartbreak
of being left out as a child on the playground or the excitement of
seeing your name on the cast list for a play or the roster of a team.
Maybe you remember getting a letter jacket in high school and
wearing it with pride to show that you were a part of something
bigger than yourself.

Similarly, initiation into the Church through Baptism brings us
into fellowship with its other members. We have companionship
and a shared purpose. But something deeper is at work, something
invisible but very real. We are not just joined to our fellow Catholics.

Being initiated into the Church means we have been brought in to the body of Christ. This is not a metaphor; it is a real, substantial union. Christian initiation makes us one with Jesus and the Church.

Consider the life of St. Paul, the great preacher of the early Church who wrote most of the New Testament. Paul was once an enemy to Christianity. He had been hunting and persecuting Christians when he was struck down from his horse on the way to Damascus. He heard a voice ask, "Saul, Saul, why do you persecute me?" Paul asked, "Who are you, sir?" and the voice responded, "I am Jesus whom you are persecuting."

Notice how Jesus identifies himself with his Church. When Paul was persecuting Christians, he was persecuting Jesus himself in his body, the Church. As we know, after this revelation, Paul converted to Christ. Seeing the Church as the Body of Christ changes one's perspective. As a famous poem often attributed to St. Teresa of Avila goes, "Christ has no body now but yours, no hands, no feet on earth but your own."

So the sacraments of initiation have amazing power. Through Baptism, we become members of Jesus' body through grace, and we are brought more fully into this body through Confirmation and through the Eucharist. The grace we receive in Christian initiation makes us more than members of a club; sacramental initiation makes us sons and daughters of God. But how does this happen?

In Baptism, water is poured upon our heads, signifying a dying to our old selves. Washed clean from sin through the power of God's grace, we emerge as children of God made one with Christ. When we receive the Eucharist—Body, Blood, Soul, and Divinity of Jesus— we become living tabernacles of Christ and carry him into the world. At Confirmation, our initiation is fulfilled, and we are empowered with unique grace to spread and defend the Faith, participating in the mission of Christ. In these sacraments, we are gifted with the greatness for which we are made.

DISCUSSION QUESTIONS

1. Aside from the sacraments, discuss an important experience of initiation in your life?

2. How does understanding the Church as the Body of Christ fit with your experience?

3. How has the Church offered you a sense of belonging? How can you as a part of Christ's body offer this sense of belonging to others?

Tips

- Look for ways to nourish your own sense of belonging to the body of Christ by offering your unique gifts to your fellow Church members. In your parish, consider becoming a lector or a catechist or assisting the work of the Church in some other capacity. If there is a ministry need that you see unfulfilled, pray about initiating it yourself!

- Many Church organizations and community groups use social media to communicate their events and activities or form online group studies, book clubs, and discussions. This might be a way for you to find new connections in the Church.

Every baptized
person should
consider that it is
in the womb of the
Church where he is
transformed from
a child of Adam to
a child of God.

St. Vincent Ferrer

Chapter Five

BAPTISM: CHILD OF GOD

Let's talk about Baptism

Do you remember when your first child was baptized? Or maybe you have been to a baptism recently. Perhaps you found the baptismal ceremony somewhat brief, with just a few prayers, the priest or deacon pouring the water, and the baby bursting into tears. It all happened so fast; what really happened in those few moments?

In short, a rebirth. Not a physical rebirth by re-entering the womb, as Nicodemus thought at first in John 3, but a rebirth of water and the Spirit, a spiritual birth in which we become children of God (see CCC 1213, 1215).

Think back to the definition of sacraments as efficacious signs. These signs have both *form* and **matter**. *Form* refers to the words, gestures, or structure of the rite. *Matter* refers to the physical "stuff" used in the sacrament. In Baptism, the form is the Trinitarian formula proclaimed by the priest or deacon as he pours the water over the recipient's head: "I baptize you in the name of the Father, and of the Son, and of the Holy Spirit." The matter is the water itself. These words convey the powerful truth that Baptism makes us sharers in the life of the Trinity and members of the body of Christ, the Church. The water signifies how this transformation takes place.

The soul is regenerated in the sacred waters of baptism and thus becomes God's child.

St. Maximilian Kolbe

Flowing water is not only about cleansing. It is also a connection to the first waters of creation, the waters of the great Flood, and even to waters of drowning. The water of Baptism is referenced again at funerals, when the priest sprinkles the casket with water and says, "In the waters of baptism [the deceased] died with Christ, may he/she now rise with him to new and everlasting life." In Christ, the baptized is plunged into death and emerges again with new life as a new creation. The sign in Baptism is efficacious, powerful, and soul-transforming.

Why do we need to be "reborn" by water and the Spirit?

Our need for rebirth stems from our being born into the state of original sin, into a wounded world. Original sin is a lost inheritance. God gifted our first parents with grace, his life in their souls, and they forfeited that grace in favor of sin. Instead of passing on the inheritance given by God, they handed on the brokenness of sin, which brought with it suffering, a tendency toward personal sin, and even death. This is nothing less than a full-scale cosmic tragedy. Without God's direct intervention, original sin would mean eternal separation from him. Thankfully, God did intervene. He became one of us in the person of Jesus, who through his life, death, and resurrection restored our inheritance lost by sin. Baptism is where that gift is given back and restored to us. In Jesus, and through the waters of Baptism, we become sons and daughters of God the Father and temples of the Holy Spirit.

What does it mean to be a child of God?

Baptism makes us children of God. Maybe this doesn't sound like anything too unusual, as we have heard this phrase used many times. Even the secular world is familiar with Christian talk about being "children of God."

But let's examine the Church's claim about Baptism. This first sacrament makes us children of God because it changes our very nature, the core of our being. We are transformed; we become sharers in God's own life. Jesus, who is fully God and fully man, experienced life on earth and even died. His death was not an accident; it was freely chosen out of love. By his death and resurrection, Jesus defeated sin and death. Because he died for us, we can now be saved from sin and live forever. When we are baptized, we plunge into Jesus' death and become one with him. This enables us also to rise with him and ultimately be with him in heaven. We become sharers in his divine life, just as he shared fully in our human life, and this makes us children of God.

The classic children's story of Pinocchio can be a helpful analogy. Pinocchio is a "living" wooden puppet, or marionette, made by Geppetto in his image. There is great love between the two, but nonetheless, they are two different kinds of beings, human and marionette, carpenter and his handiwork. The amazing part of the story is when Pinocchio becomes a *real boy*—who then shares his maker's own nature. His marionette nature is transformed into a true human nature. See any similarities to baptism? But our story is far more breathtaking than Pinocchio's story. Our story reveals a Maker who actually first becomes what he seeks to transform.

Every baptized person is a sharer of God's own life, a son or daughter of God, an heir to the kingdom of heaven. Ponder the implications of this for yourself and all of the baptized Christians with whom you interact. Ponder the implications for your relationship with God. When you greet other Christians, whether they be your mail carrier, the checkout woman at the supermarket, your child's teacher, or a stranger, you are interacting with members of a royal family, the family of God. It is an encounter with kings and queens, princes and princesses of the kingdom of heaven. You should stop and ask for autographs! When we call God "Father," we speak truth. When we pray, we cry to the Maker of the universe who is also personal and intimate with us. Jesus emphasizes this by using "*Abba*," an Aramaic term of endearment meaning "daddy," when he teaches us how to address God. This makes perfect sense, for in Baptism we become true children of God.

Just the beginning

These shockingly bold effects of Baptism are easy to miss for a few reasons. First, Baptism is most often received by infants who have done nothing but breathe, eat, and cry. Because the one being baptized usually cannot talk, walk, or even hold his or her head up, we might be tempted to think that baptism is merely a ceremony of blessing. We need to remember, however, that grace is a free and unearned gift of love. Consider that an adult who converts from a life of sin and spends much time in study and prayer in preparation for baptism has no more "earned" the sacrament than an infant. Everyone, though, whether baby or adult, is born into original sin and needs the rebirth that baptism brings.

Second, the transformation we undergo at Baptism is invisible. The newly-baptized infant doesn't emerge from the baptismal font with streams of light shooting from his or her fingers and toes. While the eternal consequences of original sin are erased as the baptized becomes one with Christ's death and resurrection, our human tug and tendency toward sin, called *concupiscence*, remains part of our earthly experience.

The transformation of Baptism may be easy to miss, but it is very real. And it is just the beginning.

DISCUSSION QUESTIONS

1. How might the truth that the baptized are sharers in God's nature affect the way you look at others? How does it affect the way you think of God as a Father?

2. How does your identity as a child of God affect how you see yourself?

Tips

- Along with birthdays, celebrate baptismal days in your family or with friends. If new life emerging at birth is worthy of celebrating, so too is the new eternal life gained through Baptism.

- When you know children being baptized, write them letters to be opened and read at their future first communions and confirmations when the initiation begun in Baptism continues to fruition.

Be who God
meant you to be
and you will set
the world on fire.

St. Catherine of Siena

Chapter Six

CONFIRMATION:
LIVE THE IMPOSSIBLE

Equipped for witness

At a recent parish event, parents whose teens were preparing for
Confirmation were asked to recall their own experience of this
sacrament. There was an awkward pause. Most of the parents
shared that they were not quite sure what they were doing or why
they were doing it when they were confirmed. They remembered
that a bishop was there, that there was oil, and that they didn't
have to go to religious education classes afterwards, but they didn't
remember much else. One of the parents at the meeting referred
to his Confirmation as "Catholic graduation." Unfortunately, this
sums up the impression of many regarding confirmation. After
the meeting, a few parents stayed behind to express the hope that
their children would be better prepared than they were. Is your
story similar? Did you recognize what was happening on the day of
your confirmation?

To understand the true power and necessity of Confirmation,
let's go back to the apostles before Pentecost. They had learned
truth firsthand from Jesus himself. They had traveled and worked
alongside him. They had witnessed his miracles, most spectacularly
the Resurrection. They had received clear instructions from Jesus
about how to live and what to do. Even so, after the Ascension, they

stopped and waited. Why? What more could they possibly have needed to stir up their faith into living action?

Their initiation as Christ's apostles had genuinely transformed them, but their transformation had not yet reached its fullness. After Jesus' ascension, they gathered to wait, prepare, and pray for direction. Suddenly a strong, driving wind rushed around them and fire appeared on their brows—it was Pentecost, the descent of the Holy Spirit (see Acts 2:1-4). Newly sealed by the Holy Spirit, they became the living Church, immediately empowered and equipped to go out and fearlessly continue Jesus' mission in the world. Confirmation, for us, does the same.

> I wish not merely to be called *Christian,* but also to be Christian.
>
> St. Ignatius of Antioch

Like Baptism, Confirmation transforms us forever. It changes us on the deepest level of our being; in sacramental language, it leaves an "indelible mark" on our souls. Confirmation fulfills the journey of Christian initiation by sending us out not merely to *do* something, but to *be* something. In confirmation, are empowered to be "soldiers" for Christ, working in the same Spirit who empowered the first Christians to share the gospel, often at the cost of their lives. These early martyrs (the word *martyr* literally means "witness") gave fearless witness to Christ even to death, joining their sacrifice to his on the cross.

Although most of us are not called to martyrdom, we are nonetheless called to witness the gospel persistently in our daily lives. Bold, joyful Christian witness is not easy. Christians remain a contradiction to the world and must often make sacrifices for their faith. The strength to make those sacrifices comes from the Holy Spirit given to us in confirmation—the same sacrament that fueled the witness of the apostles and martyrs. Confirmation seals us with the Holy Spirit so that we can become more deeply rooted in our identity as God's sons and daughters and live this identity with a boldness and joy that can, in turn, transform the world.

The form and matter of Confirmation

In Confirmation, as in all the sacraments, our senses are fully engaged. The form of Confirmation is the bishop's hand raised in anointing as he proclaims, "Be sealed with the Holy Spirit." The confirmand feels and smells the matter—sacred *chrism*, the sacramental oil used for the anointing. Working through these visible and sensory elements, the same Holy Spirit who was poured out upon the apostles at Pentecost fills the soul of the person receiving confirmation.

Whereas Baptism transforms our identity, making us God's sons and daughters, Confirmation enables us to fulfill this identity. As God's children, we are called to be living witnesses to our Father's love. To equip us for this task, Confirmation stirs up the gifts of the Holy Spirit within us. These seven gifts, which increase our power to live as witnesses for Christ, are wisdom, understanding, counsel,

> We know certainly that our God calls us to a holy life, that he gives us every grace, every abundant grace; and though we are so weak of ourselves, this grace is able to carry us through every obstacle and difficulty.
>
> *St. Elizabeth Ann Seton*

fortitude, knowledge, piety, and fear of the Lord. Our capacity for discipleship and our bond with the Church—the whole people of God—are deepened.

The movement of the Holy Spirit at Confirmation is *outward*. After Pentecost, the apostles no longer huddled in isolation but overflowed with zeal to share the gospel. In Confirmation, we are transformed and empowered to become apostles of our own time.

DISCUSSION QUESTIONS

1. What are your memories of Confirmation? How would you describe the experience?

2. Where do you see evidence of the power of the Holy Spirit at work, both in your life and in the lives of others?

Tips

- Pray a novena to the Holy Spirit in anticipation of Pentecost or leading up to some important date in your life. This is a powerful way to connect intentionally to the special relationship with the Holy Spirit established at Confirmation.

- Look for opportunities to be a missionary, even in the ordinary routine of your day. Missionaries are, above all, witnesses to Christ. You can witness by inviting others to pray, by offering small acts of service, and even by intentionally fostering joy and gratitude instead of impatience and complaining.

Do you realize that Jesus is there in the tabernacle expressly for you – for you alone? He burns with the desire to come into your heart ... don't listen to the demon, laugh at him, and go without fear to receive the Jesus of peace and love.

St. Thérèse of Lisieux

Chapter Seven

HOLY EUCHARIST: GOD WITH US

What is the Eucharist?

The Eucharist—the Body, Blood, Soul, and Divinity of Jesus—is "the source and summit" of the Church's life, the very heart of who we are as Christians (CCC 1324).[1] A few years back, a Christian musician, a non-Catholic, described his profound experience of Eucharistic adoration at a Catholic festival as "heaven crashing into earth." In the Eucharist, God comes to unite with his people, time and space are broken open, and the entire mystery of salvation is made alive and present. Heaven crashes into our ordinary everyday lives in the midst of meetings, traffic, soccer practices, and laundry. Whenever we go to Mass or make a visit to a Catholic church, the living Jesus, the king of heaven, is there to meet us.

Bread and wine become the Body, Blood, Soul, and Divinity of Jesus Christ. This truth is so profound and amazing that we might not fully realize what it means. Sit with it for a moment. Bread and wine become ... the Body and Blood of Jesus. We know this is true because of what Jesus himself said. Speaking to a crowd who had just seen him multiply five loaves to feed five thousand, he said, "I am the bread of life" (John 6:35), and, "Unless you eat the flesh of the Son of man and drink his blood, you have no life

---

[1]   *LG 11.*

in you" (John 6:53). To make it clear, he added, "My flesh is true food, and my blood is true drink" (John 6:55 NAB). Many in the crowd couldn't believe it. "This is a hard saying" (John 6:60), they responded, and they walked away, no longer following him as disciples. But Jesus did not take back what he had said. Nor did he say, "Wait a minute. You misunderstood me. I didn't really mean that *literally*." A few months later, at the Last Supper, as he blessed and broke the bread, he said to his apostles, "Take, eat; this is my body" (Matthew 26:26). Then he took the cup of wine, blessed it, and said, "Drink of it, all of you; for this is my blood of the covenant, which is poured out for many for the forgiveness of sins" (Matthew 26:27-28).

But how does this happen? At Mass, during the consecration, the priest elevates the *host* (bread) and the *chalice* (cup of wine), and, through God's power, they become the Body, Blood, Soul, and Divinity of Jesus Christ. This process is called **transubstantiation,** which means that the substances of bread and wine are replaced with the substance of Jesus' Body and Blood. "What it is" changes. While the texture, color, and taste of bread and wine remain after consecration, these are merely external qualities. After consecration, the Holy Eucharist is not bread and wine at all but the Body and Blood of Christ. This is the most radical and beautiful miracle we will experience in our lives.

> O wonderful majesty!
> What stupendous condescension!
> O sublime humility!
> O humble sublimity!
> That the Lord of the whole universe, God and the Son of God, should humble himself like this and hide under the form of a little bread, for *our salvation!*
>
> St. Francis of Assisi

Carlo Acutis, who died in 2006 at the age of fifteen, researched and compiled an exhibit highlighting more than 136 Eucharistic miracles from throughout the world. From an early stage, Carlo was captivated by what St. John Paul II called "Eucharistic amazement," and before his death he sought to draw attention to the power of the Blessed Sacrament through the many miracles that have occurred over the centuries and to this day. In each documented and approved miracle, the power of the Eucharist was highlighted in an extraordinary way. Hosts have taken on the properties of flesh, have bled, levitated, or remained impervious to fire. These miracles, reminders of the miracle that takes place at every Mass, are not simply odd occurrences worthy of *Ripley's Believe It or Not*. Rather, they are meant to awaken a sense of amazement and wonder to help us believe and receive the power of Jesus present in the Eucharist. As Carlo, at eleven, said, "The more of the Eucharist we receive, the more we will become like Jesus, so that on this earth we will have a foretaste of heaven."

The Eucharist is the living memorial of Jesus' suffering, death, and resurrection. Think of a memorial statue on a Civil War battlefield that reminds us of things that happened long ago, or a symbol such as a flag that calls to mind our country. The Eucharist is much more than a statue or a symbol. It is living. It is Jesus himself. And

> When you have received him, stir up your heart to do him homage; speak to him about your spiritual life, gazing upon him in your soul where he is present for your happiness; welcome him as warmly as possible, and behave outwardly in such a way that your actions may give proof to all of his presence.
>
> *St. Francis de Sales:*

in the Mass, the sacrifice of Jesus on the cross becomes present. The Eucharist is Christ in action, in the very act of offering himself to the Father to feed our hungry souls.

When and why we receive

All of us are hungry—starving, in fact—and we are thirsty, parched to our bones. But this is a hunger and thirst no snack bar or energy drink can satisfy. Jesus knows our hunger and thirst. When the crowd was starving after days in a deserted place, Jesus multiplied loaves and fish to feed them (see Matthew 14:13-21; Mark 6:31-44; Luke 9:12-17; John 6:1-14). But when that same crowd came to find him later, Jesus told them about a much better food that he came to give: his very flesh. The hunger of the crowd is the same hunger every person is born with—a hunger for God. We are starving for a powerful, unconditional, and eternal love that nothing in this world can offer. We are starving for grace, God's life, and Jesus gives us himself to satisfy that longing.

When we receive holy communion, we receive the Bread of Life as Jesus feeds us with himself. Communion is just that—*union with* Jesus. Since the Eucharist is not merely a symbol, St. Paul reminds us that we ought to examine our hearts and consciences before we receive (see 1 Corinthians 11:27-28.) For this reason, the Church reminds us that we need to confess any mortal sins before we receive communion. This is not about a punishment but about protecting the dignity of the Eucharist. It is about being in a right relationship with Jesus. St. Paul even says that many were sick and dying in Corinth because they were unworthily receiving the Eucharist (see 1 Corinthians 11:30). Should we fall into sin, Jesus' call to us is simple and clear: go to confession. Repair the relationship. Be healed, and return to communion!

At certain points in the history of the Church, popular piety mistakenly stressed that Catholics should seldom go to communion out of a scrupulous fear of being "unworthy" to receive. In contrast, St. Thérèse of Lisieux, talking about feelings of unworthiness and lack of confidence in God's love, says, "Receive Communion often, very often ... That is the only remedy if you want to be healed." This means that we should attend Mass often, even daily, and receive the Lord in the Eucharist.

The Liturgy of the Eucharist

Understanding the nature of the Mass can be helpful to our understanding of the Eucharist. Sometimes, you will hear the Mass referred to as the **liturgy,** a word which literally means "work of the people." Mass is an action we undertake, not merely something we observe as spectators. But what action? At Mass, we offer God our joys and sufferings, along with the work of our hands—bread and wine—so that these can become the Body and Blood of Jesus through the ministry of the priest. Boredom or apathy about Mass can be rooted in a passive attitude that expects Mass to be entertaining. But the Mass is not intended to be entertainment;

> *All* the good works in the world are not equal to the Holy Sacrifice of the Mass because they are the works of men; but the Mass is the work of God. Martyrdom is nothing in comparison for it is but the sacrifice of man to God; but the Mass is the sacrifice of God for man.
>
> *- St. John Vianney*

rather, it is the supreme way we can interact with God. Every Mass is an act of worship, a work of love, an active offering.

The word *Eucharist* means "thanksgiving." The sacrament of the Eucharist is a "thanksgiving," an "offering of thanks," to God the Father. In the Mass, Jesus offers to God the Father the same perfect sacrifice and the perfect act of love he offered on the Cross. Our simple offering of bread and wine becomes the Body and Blood of Jesus and becomes one with Jesus' ultimate sacrifice. At communion, we receive in return the sacrificial fruit: Jesus. We are united in our bodies with the living God!

Since we receive Jesus truly, not symbolically, we are united not only to him but to everyone who receives him. Through communion with Jesus, the whole congregation—in the diversity of their ages, professions, interests, personalities, races, or languages—is in communion with one another. The baptismal reality of the Church as Christ's body is fully realized at Mass, where we are truly one as his members.

After holy communion, we pray and offer thanks, receive a blessing, and are sent forth into the world with a commission: "Go in peace to love and serve the Lord!" As we have seen, the word *Mass* comes from the Latin *missa*, which means "sent." Like the apostles at Pentecost, the congregation is fueled by grace for witness in the world.

DISCUSSION QUESTIONS

1. Have you ever experienced "heaven crashing into earth?" Share your experience.

2. Is there one idea about the Eucharist that stands out to you right now? Why is it catching your attention?

3. How do you prepare for communion? How might you better prepare?

Tips

- Read about the story of the Eucharistic miracle of Lanciano, which occurred in Italy in the eighth century. Reflecting on this extraordinary event and others like it can help us better grasp the reality that the Eucharist is really Jesus.

- Spend time regularly, even if only for a few moments, in Eucharistic adoration. Silence before the Real Presence of Jesus in the Eucharist can be deeply fruitful for contemplation and spiritual growth.

- Every time he passed a tabernacle within a church, St. Francis of Assisi was said to stop and acknowledge the real presence of Jesus there with the prayer: "We adore you, Lord Jesus Christ, in this church, and we bless you, because by your holy cross you have redeemed the world." Adopting a similar habit of brief prayer when you pass a Catholic church can foster better awareness of Jesus' real presence in the Eucharist.

PART THREE

Finding God

The Lord comes to us like a physician to heal the wounds left by our sins. Tribulation is the divine medicine.

St. Augustine of Hippo

Chapter Eight

SACRAMENTS OF HEALING

Bad news, good news

First, the bad news: Sickness, suffering, and brokenness are a part of human life, along with repeated sin and failure. There, we said it. Maybe we would rather not think about it, but that does not change that we are all physically and spiritually vulnerable. Baptism and Confirmation give us an awesome and real empowerment, but they do not erase our vulnerability. It shows up in small ways like allergies and the flu and in large ways like when someone we love is diagnosed with cancer or has a tragic accident. In many ways, we are weak—both in small ways, such as being lazy or irritable with others, and in big ways, such as lying, stealing, or committing some other serious sin.

Now, on to the good news! Healing of both body and soul has been central to the ministry of Christ and his Church since the very beginning. If you need healing—and we all do—you have come to the right place. Right at the beginning of Jesus' public ministry, he sent a powerful message that he wants to heal us. Jesus was preaching in a crowded house when a paralyzed man who could not get in the doors or windows was lowered down through the roof (see Mark 2). The man's friends literally opened up the roof to lower him to Jesus for healing. To the shock of everyone, Jesus actually healed the man. But the healing had two parts: first, the forgiveness of the man's sins, and second, the healing of his physical paralysis. As God, Jesus has the authority and power to do both. This healing sets a pattern. Jesus ministers both to our bodies and our souls—to the complete person.

> All those who belong to Jesus Christ are fastened with him to the *Cross.*
>
> St. Augustine

In the climax of Jesus' ministry at the crucifixion, something truly revolutionary happened to human suffering and healing. On the Cross, Jesus' suffering became the means of our redemption, the pathway to the forgiveness of sin, and the healing of our ultimate vulnerability to death. When Jesus suffered and died, he changed the very meaning of suffering. Suffering is no longer empty or fruitless anymore but can be the route to healing. When we are ill, lonely, or grieving, our sufferings can be joined to his and become means for healing, too.

Throughout the history of the Church, we can find many examples of bodily healing, both natural and miraculous, where a person's suffering is ended. But we also find thousands of examples where God permits suffering to draw us into deeper union with Jesus. Following Jesus doesn't give us a way *out* of suffering. Rather, faith in Christ is a way *into* suffering, so that it can be redemptive. Whatever we face in life, nothing can rob us of the peace we have through faith.

From the early Church to today, the ministry of healing continues through social ministries, healthcare services, and many other outreaches that serve people's physical needs. But Jesus' ministry of healing, both spiritually and physically, continues most profoundly through the healing sacraments of Reconciliation and Anointing of the Sick. Here, we will focus on these two sacraments.

Often called confession, the sacrament of Reconciliation ministers to us the way that Jesus ministered to the paralyzed man: first, by healing the brokenness of our souls. Through Reconciliation, our sins are forgiven by Jesus' saving power. In the Anointing of the Sick, we call upon Christ's power to heal and unite the sufferings of the ill person with Jesus' suffering on the cross. Regardless of whether physical healing occurs, this sacrament strengthens us in our illness and helps our suffering be redemptive.

In both sacraments, the healing comes through a relationship with Jesus and with his Church. All of Jesus' healing miracles came with an invitation to a deeper relationship with God. More than anything else, true healing is found in experiencing God's love. Reconciliation isn't just a technicality, like paying a fine. Anointing of the Sick isn't just a nice gesture. Both are real encounters with Jesus, who loves us and calls us above all to deeper relationship and intimacy. In the next two segments, we will look at how the sacraments of healing accomplish this mission.

> During painful times, when you feel a terrible void, think how the capacity of your soul is being enlarged so that it can receive God—becoming as it were, infinite as God is infinite.
>
> *St. Elizabeth of the Trinity*

DISCUSSION QUESTIONS

1. Reflect on any areas of your life that need deeper healing. Discuss any examples you feel comfortable sharing with the group.

2. Do you know someone who intentionally joined his or her pain to Jesus' suffering on the cross? What has struck you about this person's "redemptive suffering"?

Earth has no sorrow that *heaven* cannot heal.

St. Thomas More

> *Suffering* is nothing by itself. But suffering shared with the passion of Christ is a wonderful gift, the most beautiful gift, a token of love.
>
> – *St. Teresa of Calcutta (Mother Teresa)*

Tips

- Approach God eagerly and persistently for healing, like the friends of the paralyzed man. They tore off a roof just to get him to Jesus! There is nothing too big—or too small—for God. The exercise of journaling about these needs can be fruitful in receiving his healing love.

- Following the example of countless saints, whenever you feel a complaint forming, try to "offer up" that moment as a sacrifice to Jesus. The habit of offering up our ordinary frustrations and everyday stresses can help open us to see suffering in a new light.

Confession is an act of honesty and courage – an act of entrusting ourselves, beyond sin, to the mercy of a loving and forgiving God.

St. John Paul II

Chapter Nine

CONFESSION: WHERE SAINTS ARE MADE

Jesus knew we would need forgiveness

Think back again to that paralytic man in Mark 2. Amazingly, many people present were outraged that Jesus forgave the man's sins instead of being moved by his miraculous healing of the man's paralysis. "Only God can forgive sins," they complained. Actually, in these words, they were revealing great truth. Only God *can* forgive sins … so Jesus could forgive only *because he is God*, the Second Person of the Trinity. That might be easy to accept if Jesus were standing before you and saying the words of forgiveness. But what about a priest in the sacrament of reconciliation? He clearly is not God. How, then, can he forgive our sins?

This is a good question, one that takes us back to the apostles. One night after the Resurrection, they were gathered in a locked room when suddenly Jesus walked through the walls to join them. He then breathed on them, bestowing them with the authority to forgive sins in his name by the power of the Holy Spirit (see John 20:22-23). So when we go to confession, the priest absolves us from our sins through this same authority Jesus gave the apostles and their successors, the bishops. The priest forgives, but only with the power God has given him.

Jesus gave this sacramental power to the apostles, the first bishops, who conferred it on their successors. Jesus gave the Church this gift because he knew we would need it. Baptism transforms our identity and destiny, but it does not eliminate our tendency toward sin or the brokenness with which we all struggle. Jesus provided a tangible way for us to express repentance, to receive the assurance of forgiveness, and to be empowered to avoid future sin.

But what do I need to do to seek God's forgiveness in the sacrament of Reconciliation?

Contrition

First, we need to approach Reconciliation with the right attitude. The essential attitude for a good confession is fairly straightforward: sorrow for our sins and a firm resolution to change (also known as a "firm purpose of amendment"). But what if you find yourself confessing the same sins every time? What if your confession today is exactly the same as the last confession? Does this mean you are not really sorry for your sins? Does it mean you are not really trying to change?

These questions are natural and helpful, but they also sometimes mislead our expectations regarding *contrition* (sorrow for sin). Sincere contrition isn't determined by our emotions or our passions. Contrition is a decision to reject sin and choose God, even if we have to do so over and over again. Due to the power of habit and personal weakness, we may find ourselves regularly committing the same sins. Reconciliation requires only that we make an act of the will—a choice—to reject sin and resolve to avoid sin going forward. We make this choice concrete by giving some thought to the situations that lead us into sin and plan to avoid those situations.

We should never tire of returning to God for the forgiveness and freedom he never tires of offering us in this sacrament.

Examination of conscience

Sorrow for our sins—contrition—is the first step, but what if we are unsure of the specific sins we committed? To help us here, we make an *examination of conscience*, which is a thoughtful reflection on our sinful thoughts, actions, or omissions since our previous confession. We ask the Holy Spirit to help us recall and repent of our sins. In fact, one of the Holy Spirit's primary actions is to "convict" us of sin (see John 16:8). But don't confuse "convict" with "condemn." Condemnation beats down our spirit, lays on heavy shame or guilt, and degrades our dignity. This is never the operation of the Holy Spirit. Instead, conviction clearly presents the truth of our actions. Seeing this truth motivates us to be free from our particular sins. Conviction is always ordered toward healing. The Holy Spirit convicts us in the necessary and healthy way that a mechanic might pop open a car hood to identify and correct the problem.

There are many examinations of conscience you could use. Basically, they all help us reflect on what we have done that violates the commandments or damages our relationship with God and others. The "best" examination of conscience is the one that is effective at helping you pinpoint serious sins that require healing. Some find it fruitful

> Confession is the soul's bath. You must go at least once a week. I do not want souls to stay away from confession more than a week. Even a clean and unoccupied room gathers dust; return after a week and you will see that it needs dusting again!
>
> *St. Pio of Pietrelcina (Padre Pio)*

to complete their examination by making a written list to bring into confession.

Then, go to confession, either when it is regularly offered (typically on Saturday afternoons) or by making an appointment with a priest. It can sometimes be a struggle to stop postponing or avoiding this healing sacrament.

The courage to go to confession

Since your previous confession, the weeks turned into months, and then months to a year, and then a year into five years … and now you can't even remember what to do or say. Some stay away from confession because they feel awkward, maybe partly because of their sins and partly because they simply don't know what to do anymore in this sacrament. At Mass, it is fairly easy to follow along and blend in with the congregation, but confession can seem like an intimidating "solo" performance. But don't let fear of forgetting some words keep you from the freedom of forgiveness!

Remember: You are not actually "on your own" in confession. The priest is there to help you. One man shared that when he returned to confession after a decade, he braced himself for a reprimand from the priest for being away from the sacrament for so long. Much to his surprise, the priest just warmly said, "Welcome back!" Then he gently guided the man through the steps that he had long forgotten. Priests actually look forward to welcoming people back to confession after many years. As one priest put it, "They are my big fish. They remind me of why I became a priest in the first place."

Maybe you go to confession regularly. Maybe your confession story is more about frustration with repeating the same sins every time, or wanting the experience to be more meaningful. No matter how often you go or what sins you confess, you are a sinner loved by God … and Jesus wants to heal and love you through the sacrament of reconciliation. Each of us can benefit from looking more deeply into what this sacrament does and how it works.

Celebrating the sacrament of Reconciliation

Normally, we receive the sacrament of Reconciliation in a reconciliation room or a traditional "confessional," usually located in the rear of a church or in the vestibule. The priest will already be there waiting. When you enter, you can choose to confess "face-to-face" with the priest or to kneel behind a screen. Begin by saying, "Bless me, Father, for I have sinned. It has been *[approximate amount of time]* since my last confession." If you feel unsure about what to do, just say: "Father, I don't really know what to do." He will help you through the necessary steps.

Next, based on the examination of conscience you made, confess your sins, both in kind and number. That is, confess what you have done and how many times you have done it, as well as you can remember. Extreme details and precision aren't necessary; simply try to summarize your sins and how frequently you committed each. You must confess any mortal sins—i.e., those sins that involve serious matter and are done with full knowledge and consent.

When you have finished your confession, the priest may offer some counsel to help you to heal and avoid repeating these sins. After this, he will prescribe to you a penance.

Receiving a penance

The sacrament of Reconciliation wipes away the consequences of mortal sin— i.e., separation from God in hell. But sin also has practical, real-world effects that require some kind of reparation. To be clear: penance is not *how* our sins are forgiven, like some kind of trade deal or barter with God. Forgiveness of sins is a free gift of grace that only God can accomplish. Penance is an action we are given by the priest to help us make things right, to repair some of the damage we have done by our sins.

The priest will consider your particular situation and state in life when prescribing an appropriate penance. Common penances are reciting certain prayers, doing an act of service, or some other sacrificial action related to your confession. Fulfilling the penance is a required element of the sacrament.

Act of contrition

After he prescribes a penance, the priest will invite you to make an act of contrition. This is a prayer that expresses your decision to reject sin, to avoid near occasions of sin, and to strive to avoid sinning in the future. There are several variations of the act of contrition, and you can use your own words. Here is a traditional form:

> *O my God, I am heartily sorry for having offended you, and I detest all my sins because of your just punishments, but most of all because they offend you, my God, who are all-good and deserving of all my love. I firmly resolve, with the help of your grace to sin no more and to avoid the near occasions of sin.*

Absolution

After praying an act of contrition, the priest will then absolve you from your sins. This is the *form* of the sacrament, the moment at which your sins are definitively forgiven by the priest acting *in persona Christi Capitis* ("in the person of Christ the Head")—that is, with the authority of Christ given him by the Church. (The *matter* of the sacrament is the sins that have been confessed.) The priest raises his hand and speaks the following profound words of mercy:

> *God, the Father of mercies, through the death and resurrection of his Son has reconciled the world to himself and sent the Holy Spirit among us for the forgiveness of sins; through the ministry of the Church may God give you pardon and peace, and I absolve you from your sins in the name of the Father, and of the Son, and of the Holy Spirit.*

In speaking these words, as mentioned, the priest is acting in the "person of Christ." Through the ministry of the priest, through the power of the Holy Spirit, Christ continues his mission of healing and reconciliation—just as he did with the paralytic in the Gospels. Lucky for us, we don't have to pull off a roof to get to Jesus! The reconciliation room has easily accessible doors, and all we have to do to receive God's mercy is open them and walk in.

> *The* person of the priest is, for me, only a screen. Never analyze what sort of a priest it is that I am making use of; open your soul in confession as you would to me, and I will fill it with my light.
>
> *- Jesus to St. Faustina in her Divine Mercy revelations*

DISCUSSION QUESTIONS

1. Discuss a memorable instance of forgiveness you have experienced, witnessed, or heard of. Why was it so powerful?

2. What has your experience of confession been?

3. What connections do you see between forgiveness and freedom?

Tips

- Many saints recommend making an examination of conscience at the end of every day. Since most of our sins creep up in ordinary life, the habit of reviewing our daily choices can help pinpoint areas that need change.

- Regularly receiving the sacrament of Reconciliation from the same priest has many benefits. As he becomes more familiar with your unique individual circumstances, he can offer increasingly more tailored and meaningful spiritual direction.

Give yourself fully to God. He will use you to accomplish great things on the condition that you believe much more in his love than in your weakness.

St. Teresa of Calcutta (Mother Teresa)

Chapter Ten

ANOINTING OF THE SICK

What is the Anointing of the Sick?

When we study how Jesus interacted with those around him, we can see a pattern. He has a special tenderness for the sick, suffering, and dying. Nearly all of his public miracles involve people struggling with serious, chronic health issues. In fact, the people who pursued Jesus most fervently were the ones facing a medical crisis: lepers, parents of dying children, blind and paralyzed men, a woman with a chronic hemorrhage. Why was this?

Think about your own experience with illness. Maybe you have been through a serious illness or accident or battle a chronic condition. Maybe you have been close to someone who has experienced illness. Sickness has a way of cutting through the trivialities of everyday life and revealing just how much we need Someone greater than ourselves. Our Catholic Faith does not romanticize suffering. Suffering is real and painful, and—if we let it—can make us impatient, depressed, or even bitter. Yet maybe you have witnessed suffering's potential to refine a person's perspective and priorities.

The sacrament of Anointing of the Sick extends special grace to those who are physically suffering, very ill, or in danger of death. Where sickness takes a heavy toll, the grace of anointing gives us the strength to endure it meaningfully and even joyfully.

Some of the most powerful witnesses to faith in God's love
are credible precisely because of their response to sickness. St.
Bernadette suffered tuberculosis. St. Damien battled leprosy. Bl.
Margaret of Castello endured blindness, deafness, and severe
physical deformities. St. Ann Shaffer spent most of her life an invalid
burn victim. The father of St. Thérèse of Lisieux, St. Louis Martin,
struggled with dementia. St. John Paul II endured Parkinson's
disease. Many of us have witnesses who are even closer to us.

One evening, a parish music minister was approached after Mass
by a woman who had a friend dying of cancer. Her friend was in
hospice, and she was expected to pass away within the next two
weeks. The woman relayed the message that her dying friend
wanted the music minister to sing at her funeral. She asked if he
could meet with her to discuss possible songs, and to pray and sing
them together with friends. He accepted her invitation. He was
astounded that this dying woman was concerned that the music
uplift her friends, point them toward prayer, and offer hope and
healing. They made arrangements to meet in a few days.

When the music minister arrived, a priest was on his way out. He
had just administered the anointing of the sick. The music minister
nervously unlatched his guitar case, greeted the guests, and handed
out song sheets. His nervousness changed to amazement as they
all sang, prayed, and marveled at the heroic witness of a woman
hopefully and prayerfully meeting pain and death. Undoubtedly
her witness left a permanent impression on many.

Anointing of the Sick calls out for physical healing, which God has
the power to accomplish. The sacrament's main action, however, is
bestowing the grace that helps the sick person continually unite
his or her sufferings with those of Jesus. When this happens, real
beauty can be made out of suffering and sorrow.

How is this sacrament celebrated?

In the Anointing of the Sick, the priest anoints the hand of the sick
person with oil blessed by the bishop and offers prayers for an

outpouring of grace. As the circumstances permit, confession and Eucharist are also offered to the recipient.

The form of the sacrament has been the same since the early Church. In James 5, we can see directions for priests to anoint sick members of the Church and pray for their healing and perseverance.

Who should receive the sacrament?

Prior to the Second Vatican Council, this sacrament was officially known as Extreme Unction (meaning "final anointing") and was commonly referred to as "last rites." It was understood to be a sacrament for those who were close to death. Many even today mistake it as a sacrament only for the dying. So it is no wonder that some, especially older Catholics, are reluctant to receive it!

While those in danger of death should certainly receive Anointing of the Sick, anyone facing serious or chronic illness, as well as anyone preparing for major surgery, is a proper recipient of this sacrament as well. In fact, in the case of a chronic or persistent medical condition, a person can receive the sacrament several times. There is no such thing as too much grace, especially for the challenge of persevering through chronic or painful suffering.

He did not say you would not be troubled, you would not be tempted, you would not be distressed, but he did say you would not be overcome.

St. Josemaria Escriva

DISCUSSION QUESTIONS

1. Do you know anyone who experienced physical or spiritual healing through this sacrament?

2. Do you know anyone who witnessed powerfully about God's love through their sickness?

Tips

- If you are seeking anointing for yourself or a loved one, any priest can administer the sacrament. You do not need to receive it from a priest of your parish. Hospitals usually have priests on call for patients who request this sacrament.

- You might think that all the "good" miracles happened in biblical times. But you are loved *right now* by the same Jesus who miraculously raised people from the dead and healed lifelong illnesses in an instant. Never be afraid to ask him for a miracle! He is no less able or willing to perform miracles than he has ever been.

PART FOUR

Service for God

I am definitively loved, and whatever happens to me, I am awaited by this love. And so my life is good!

St. Josephine Bakhita

Chapter Eleven

SACRAMENTS OF SERVICE

Service and self-gift

Imagine the scene: the apostles and Jesus had gathered to eat and pray when Jesus got down on his knees and started washing their feet. In the days of muddy roads shared with donkeys and camels, this was a common measure of courtesy, typically performed by slaves or servants. Can you imagine how taken aback the apostles were? Why was their rabbi, their Master, literally lowering himself to do such a common, repugnant task? Wasn't such a thing beneath his dignity?

Jesus was aware of their thoughts, so when he had finished washing, he said, "For I have given you an example, that you also should do as I have done to you" (John 13:15). The example was the gift of oneself humbly for the good of another. The example was love as service.

Love as service and self-gift takes special meaning and priority in the "sacraments of service": Holy Orders and Matrimony. These two sacraments have a common purpose. Both commit individuals to offer a lifelong self-gift for the good of others. In both sacraments, the gift of self is meant to follow the example of Jesus, who offers his very self for the salvation of those whom he loves. For those called into them, these two sacraments are missions to wash the feet of others.

What does this mean? Sometimes, for a priest, it means hours spent in the confessional healing the burdens of hurting souls. On a large teen retreat, a parish youth minister realized that a newly ordained priest had been hearing confessions for seven hours, with no breaks as far as he could tell. When the line finally dried up and the priest came to dinner, the youth minister looked at his bleary eyes and asked, "Are you OK?" The enthusiastic priest smiled and responded, "Are you kidding? I live for this!" In marriage, washing feet might mean waking up before your spouse to make coffee, giving up the remote, swallowing your pride, or even literally washing things on your hands and knees. When hard times strike, it could mean a host of completely unpredictable things. In both cases though, the call is clear—to serve and lay down one's life.

> *For love* to be real, it must empty us of self.
>
> St. Teresa of Calcutta (Mother Teresa)

Mission flows from identity. When we know who we are, once we are confirmed in this identity, we can confidently undertake our mission. We see this first in Jesus' life. First came his baptism. Then came the outpouring of the Holy Spirit upon him and the voice of God the Father confirming Jesus' identity: "This is my beloved Son; with whom I am well pleased" (Matthew 3:17). Jesus' public mission followed this preparation.

Notice that the sacraments flow from this pattern. First, the sacraments of initiation bring us into the Church, making us children and heirs. Then, the sacraments of healing continually sustain and repair us. Finally, equipped with these graces, we are given a mission to fulfill in the sacraments of service.

The primary objective of both Holy Orders and Matrimony is self-giving service that helps others become holy and get to heaven and that offers public witness. Though we may not usually think of it this way, marriage is as much a call to service as the priesthood. Both sacraments share precisely the same mission to mirror the self-giving love of Christ to the Church.

There are a few distinctions, of course. In Holy Orders, ordained ministers—bishops, priests, and deacons—offer themselves to serving the needs of the Church, especially through administrating the sacraments. Married couples, through the unconditional faithfulness that they vowed to each other, are a public witness to God's unconditional love and fidelity to us. The life-giving love of spouses is an image of the life-giving love of the Trinity, and, quite literally, married life is service. Husbands and wives, fathers and mothers, find themselves alongside Jesus on their hands and knees—where washing feet might be cleaning up spilled Cheerios or picking up dirty socks off the floor.

> Love and sacrifice are as intimately connected as sun and light. We cannot love without suffering or suffer without loving.
>
> *St. Gianna Molla*

> *To* love a person means ... being prepared to change and to suffer, to renounce something for them.
>
> *– Blessed Chiara Corbella Petrillo*

> *Our* body is a cenacle, a monstrance: through its crystal the world should see God.
>
> *– St. Gianna Molla*

DISCUSSION QUESTIONS

1. Are you surprised to learn that the sacraments of Holy Orders and Matrimony have so much in common? Discuss.

2. How do you personally hear God calling you to mission? In what ways and places do you "hear" his voice?

Teach us ... to *give* and not to count the cost.

St. Ignatius of Loyola

Tips

- Most of us could include more service in our schedules if we made a real, honest effort. You don't need to reinvent the wheel; simply look for existing service opportunities that appeal to you. Maybe it is a monthly shift at the local food bank or soup kitchen. Maybe it is some ministry in your parish. Maybe it is volunteering at your children's school. The spirit of service can flourish when we simply turn good intentions into real-life commitments.

- We see the saints repeatedly recommending small, ordinary acts of service as the path to great holiness. Silencing a complaint or criticism; bringing a hot cup of coffee; completing some mundane chore so someone else won't have to--these are all treasures of service. Even saints with extraordinary missions such as St. Teresa of Calcutta said that authentic service always begins with those around us. Reflect on the small ways that you might serve your family and co-workers more intentionally today. As St. Josemaria Escriva reminds us, "Do everything for Love. Thus there will be no little things: everything will be big."

People who say that we priests are lonely ... have gotten it all wrong ... We are in love with Love, with the Author of Love!

St. Josemaria Escriva

Chapter Twelve

HOLY ORDERS: THE POWER OF THE PRIESTHOOD

What is Holy Orders?

Three years is the tiniest drop in the ocean of history. Yet in only three years, Jesus accomplished his entire public ministry—all the miracles, the teachings, his death and resurrection, the establishment of the Church. Although he had the power to do so, Jesus did not carry out his ministry alone. Instead, he chose a motley crew to accompany him as sharers in his work. They included fishermen, rabbinical school flunk-outs, and even a hated tax collector. But Jesus called them to be his own, to be his apostles (which literally means "one who is sent"), to sit at his feet to learn from him.

The apostles were with him as he healed the lepers, the blind, the deaf, and the lame. They interacted alongside him with public sinners, curious crowds, and constantly hostile authorities. They experienced impossible things at his command, such as feeding a few loaves and fishes to thousands or walking across water. Imagine what it must have been like to have such intimacy with Jesus!

Jesus founded the Church through this ragtag band of apostles, entrusting them and their successors with the mission of extending grace—his life and presence—to the world after his ascension into heaven. They were the first bishops, and their ministry itself is a compelling testimony to the divine origin of the Church. Remember, these were the same men (except for John) who ran away from him when he was arrested and crucified. On their own, they surely could never have dreamed up, founded, and then sustained such an organization as the Church. But the outpouring of the Holy Spirit at Pentecost transformed them into something greater than merely weak, fearful men. From then on, they eagerly and unceasingly proclaimed the gospel, even though it cost nearly all of them their lives.

The ministerial priesthood was established by Jesus at the Last Supper, when he commanded his apostles to celebrate the Eucharist in memory of him. In turn, the apostles passed on the priesthood to the next generation, who then passed it to the next and the next in an unbroken line of succession. This unbroken, directly traceable line through two millennia is itself an extraordinary and remarkable thing unlikely to be the result of mere human efforts. In the first century, the apostles chose priests (or *presbyters*, as they are referred to in the New Testament) and deacons to assist them in their ministry. So, in a nutshell, the sacrament of holy orders was established by Jesus to continue his sacramental ministry on earth until the end of time.

In the Old Testament, the Levitical priesthood was charged with the offering of sacrifice to atone for the sins of the people. So it should not be surprising that the Catholic priesthood also centers on the offering of sacrifice—the one, true sacrifice of the Eucharist at Mass, when the priest acts *in persona Christi*. When an individual priest offers the sacraments of Eucharist or reconciliation, *it is Jesus' own offering* that is made present. Through that unbroken line of priests from Peter forward, Jesus' public ministry wasn't a brief three-year run, after all—it has actually been continuing for more than two thousand years.

The priesthood, foreshadowed and fulfilled

Jesus is the fulfillment of salvation history. The events of the Old Testament were a foreshadowing of who Jesus would be and what he would do. These Old Testament prototypes were fulfilled only with the coming of Jesus.

When God called the Israelites out of slavery in Egypt, he called them to be a nation of priests—that is, to be a people who offer sacrifice to the true God. The tribe of Levi was further set apart for "ministerial priesthood" to carry out the sacrificial offerings. This parallels how all members of the Church—who form the "priesthood of all believers" by virtue of their baptism—participate in the sacrifice of Mass, which is actually celebrated by a ministerial (i.e., ordained) priest.

A key Old Testament foreshadowing of priesthood is Melchizedek, the king of Salem, who mysteriously shows up in the presence of Abraham and offers a sacrifice of bread and wine. This is a clear prefiguration of the priesthood of Christ.

None of these prototype priests, however, had the ability to offer what is required for true sanctification: a perfect, eternal sacrifice. Broken by sin, no human person could ever make a perfect offering—and the blood of animals certainly couldn't

The priest is not a priest for himself; he does not give himself absolution; he does not administer the sacraments to himself. He is not for himself, he is for you.

St. John Vianney

do it. Only Jesus, the eternal high priest and God-man, could offer the perfect sacrifice—his very body on the Cross. Through the sacrament of holy orders, priests are the instrument of Jesus continuing to make his perfect offering of himself for our salvation.

All of this may seem somewhat mysterious and distant. But Catholic priests are actually not distant at all. Think about how they are present at the most critical moments of life. When we have children, when we celebrate, when we are sick, or when we mourn death, the priest accompanies us. More profoundly, the priest offers us the sacraments that allow us to encounter Jesus. The priest continues Jesus' public ministry in every place, for every person.

The different "degrees" of Holy Orders

The sacrament of Holy Orders has this name because it encompasses three "degrees" or orders of participation in the ministry of Christ. With each degree, an ordained man becomes part of a distinct order. Here are the three orders, from "lowest" to "highest" in rank:

Deacons: The word *deacon* comes from a Greek word which means "servant." The first deacons were commissioned specifically to care for the practical needs of the Church through direct service (see Acts 6:1-7). All priests are first ordained as deacons, but some deacons remain in this order permanently— we refer to these men as *permanent deacons*. Since they have not been ordained to the priesthood, deacons cannot minister the sacraments of Reconciliation, Eucharist, Confirmation, or Anointing of the Sick. Their primary ministry involves proclaiming the Gospel at Mass, preaching, and assisting the priest at Mass, as well as celebrating the sacraments of Baptism and Matrimony and presiding over funerals. They have a particular calling to the charitable mission of the Church. Like priests, deacons serve in a particular diocese and take a promise of obedience to the bishop of the diocese.

Priests: Priests might be described as the "bishop's assistants." In the early days of the Church, as the number of Christians grew rapidly, the apostles and their successors realized that they needed help. They chose presbyters (priests) to assist them in celebrating the sacraments, particularly the Eucharist (see Acts 14:23 and Titus 1:5). Within their diocese, they act on the bishop's behalf as the "ordinary" minister of all of the sacraments except for Confirmation (which they do administer in an "extraordinary" way at the Easter Vigil) and Holy Orders, which are reserved the bishop. There are two "types" of priests—diocesan and religious. Diocesan priests are ordained for service in a particular diocese and make solemn promises of obedience to their bishop and of celibacy (though there are some married diocesan priests in different rites of the Church). Religious priests are members of religious orders and take solemn vows of poverty, chastity, and obedience.

Bishops: Bishops possess the fullest degree of priesthood of Christ, as successors to the apostles. Bishops are the ministers of Confirmation and Holy Orders, as well as any of the other sacraments. Bishops are ordained by other bishops (or by the pope), after being chosen for this sacred office by the pope himself.

A bishop who has been selected by the pope to govern a diocese is known as an *ordinary*, to distinguish him from any *auxiliary bishops* who might be assisting him. The ordinary of an archdiocese is referred to as an *archbishop*, but there is no sacramental distinction between a bishop and an archbishop.

A bishop is the shepherd of his diocese, leading his flock in its journey with the Lord. Jesus spoke of himself as the "good shepherd" (see John 10), and in his dialogue with Peter after the resurrection, he handed on the shepherd's mantle to the apostles with the command, "Feed my sheep" (John 21:17).

Celibacy for the kingdom

The one fact that everyone, both Catholics and non-Catholics alike, knows about priesthood is that priests are celibate—at least in the Roman rite of the Church. Celibacy is voluntary abstinence from marriage, so this includes abstaining from all sexual activity. The world is often fascinated with such a choice, one that seems inconceivable and impossible, and celibacy is often mocked as being absurd. What's the point? Why don't priests get married?

> The world looks to the priest, because it looks to Jesus! No one can see Christ; but everyone sees *the priest,* and through him they wish to catch a glimpse of the Lord!
>
> St. John Paul II

While celibacy "fits" with the priesthood, it is not strictly necessary or essential to the nature of the priesthood. It is a Church discipline (or law). In the history of the Church, there were married priests. Even today in some rites of the Church, married men can be ordained priests. But celibacy is the norm in the Roman rite, which is by far the largest rite of the Church. Celibacy follows the pattern set by Jesus, who was himself celibate—giving himself not to one woman but to the entire Church as his bride. Through celibacy, a priest can offer himself to the Church in an undivided way. At a moment's notice, a celibate priest is free to run to the hospital in the middle of the night or counsel a person in need for hours. Rather than committing his love to a single person in marriage, in celibacy a priest gains the freedom to love *any* person.

The ultimate reason for celibacy reaches deeper than practical logistics. Standing in the person of Christ, the celibate priest signifies the spousal relationship between Christ and the Church. He is a living, breathing sign of the heavenly union between God and his people.

Male priesthood

Maybe you have also wondered about that other obvious fact about those who receive Holy Orders—they are all men. You might have heard all kinds of questions about this reality: Is the Church outdated? Is the Church sexist? Are women less qualified or worthy than men? Could the "rules" ever change? The answer to all of these questions, is no.

The priesthood is different from careers, positions of service, and offices of leadership that depend upon personal traits and competence. It may be easy to see male priesthood as just another way women face unjust limitation, unless we recognize that the priesthood is something entirely different from any human institution.

By ordaining only men, the Church is following the instructions of Jesus himself. Jesus never degraded the dignity of women, yet he chose only men as his apostles. Some argue that Jesus did this because of his male-dominated culture, which—like nearly every other culture of the time—heavily subjugated women. But Jesus actually repeatedly ignored many of his society's cultural taboos against interacting with women, particularly those most disenfranchised of all—prostitutes and adulterers. He was never afraid to go against the norms in how he treated women, so it is unlikely that he would choose cultural conformity as a reason for establishing a male-only priesthood.

Jesus publically elevated women and affirmed their dignity during his ministry. After the Resurrection, he revealed himself first to female disciples, signifying the critical role of women in the Church. He gave a woman—his mother, Mary—the highest position in all of creation. But he did not choose women as his apostles. Therefore, the Church does not have the authority to change what Jesus established. As the *Catechism* states, "No one has a *right* to receive the sacrament of Holy Orders. Indeed no one claims this office for himself; he is called to it by God[1] ... This sacrament can be *received* only as an unmerited gift" (CCC 1578).

The priesthood also flows from the realities of human nature and gender itself. Women and men are equal before God yet different from each other. Each man and woman becomes *more* precious by acknowledging his or her uniqueness and difference. Both men and women, with their differences and individual strengths, compose a beautiful image of God. Equality before God should not be misunderstood as sameness, for sameness would diminish the uniqueness of being created as male and female.

But what does all of this have to do with male-only priesthood? When we say Jesus is true man, we mean not only that he wholly shares the human experience but also that he was incarnate as a man. To be wholly *in persona Christi*, priests must image Christ not merely in his personality traits, preferences, or talents, but also in his body.

---

[1]   *Cf. Heb 5:4.*

DISCUSSION QUESTIONS

1. Who is a priest you've heard of or know who really embodies the love of God? How does he do this?

2. What do you see as some of the unique challenges and unique joys of priesthood?

3. How do the sacraments of Holy Orders and Matrimony interact and support each other?

Tips

- Buy a priest a beer! Or do something with a priest that acknowledges his need for friendship and human intimacy. Priests are supported and sustained in the ceaseless demands of their ministry by these acts of love and companionship.

- "Adopt" a priest to pray for. Gather names of the priests serving in your area and assign a day to pray especially for each one. Pray for his vocation, his ministry, and his personal needs. You may even wish to send a card informing him of this spiritual support—no doubt he will be touched and deeply grateful.

- Interact more with those in religious life. This could mean volunteering with a religious order or making a retreat under the guided direction of a priest.

- Attend a diocesan ordination Mass, which is often held in May or June at the cathedral church of a diocese. It is a powerful experience to witness men lie prostrate before the altar as they offer themselves in service to the people of God.

Those who are called to the married state will, with the grace of God, find within their state everything they need to be holy.

St. Josemaria Escriva

Chapter Thirteen

MARRIAGE: LOVING FOR LIFE

What is the sacrament of Matrimony?

Poor, lonely Adam. Even with perfect weather in a perfectly
beautiful garden filled with a host of amazing creatures, he never
felt ... *right.* Who could he really, *really* give himself to? Who could
be a true companion? None of the animals could be; none was
his equal, so he could never share a true exchange or communion
with them.

God then placed Adam into a deep sleep and created someone who
was able to choose him as a true and equal partner, someone who
was able to receive the gift of himself that he longed to give and
offer her own self in return. When Adam awoke, he saw a woman,
human like himself but different from him. Paradoxically, Eve's
differences made Adam feel more fully himself. Together, their
complementarity formed an icon of God's love in the Trinity. Given
in free self-gift, their complementarity had the power to bring forth
new life. Their love became the dawn of the human family.

Then, despite the fullness of their joy, they gave in to sin. Adam
failed his bride and Eve failed her bridegroom when they chose to
sin. The effect of their sin was immediate and devastating. They hid
themselves from God, and they began to turn away from each other
in self-preoccupation. Their sin brought death.

The carnage of sin spread across creation like nuclear fallout. But the gifts of God were not entirely destroyed. Although the sinful distortions of fornication and adultery existed, the precious gift of marriage and family endured. When Jesus came, he established the sacrament of Matrimony to give married couples the strength to live marriage as God intended it to be.

In Ephesians 5, St. Paul explains why marriage is so critical—marriage is our primary icon of Christ's love for the Church. When we look to marriage, we can see an image of how Jesus gives himself to us and how we receive him. When we look to Jesus, we can see the model that marriage should follow. This parallel makes marriage an analogy—not an identical copy but a deeply helpful analogy—of the union between Christ and his Church.

Jesus often used this analogy, referring to himself as the Bridegroom who would lay down his life for his bride, the Church. He described heaven as a wedding feast. Most powerfully, Jesus freely, totally, and faithfully pours out his life-giving love. This pattern of unconditional, irrevocable, sacrificial love is the core of sacramental marriage.

Practically speaking

Now let's shift from this heady, sublime vision of marriage to the nitty-gritty of daily life. There are thermostat debates, sit downs over cover hogging, and a gallon of milk in the back of the fridge with only a few drops left. Then there is adjustment to little idiosyncrasies and quirks that don't seem as charming as they used to. And there are deeper issues like deeply grooved patterns of coping, conflict resolution, and childhood wounds that couples bring into their marriages. Marriage doesn't unfold in a constant shower of roses and candlelight. After they float blissfully down the aisle, spouses quickly confront the reality that they are broken. They are prone to selfishness. They are weak. They must repeatedly ask forgiveness and rededicate themselves to sacrifice. But because they love each other, they have the incentive over and over, on thousands of days in mundane circumstances, to make the gift of self once again. From this choice follows sanctification. This is the grace of marriage that Jesus had in mind.

Grace works much more like a slow cooker than like a microwave. Marriage might be the slowest cooker of all. For a married couple, the grace of every other sacrament is received within the context of marriage—the romance, the hardships, the raising of children, the upkeep of a household, the process of aging, the sickness, the health, the prosperity, the poverty. Slowly, surely, over a lifetime together, those graces transform the spouses. Love is refined and perfected as, together, the spouses travel toward heaven.

How does the sacrament work?

Matrimony is the only sacrament that is administered by those receiving it. Unlike the other sacraments, marriage is witnessed by the priest or deacon but not conferred by him. The spouses' exchange of vows is the form of the sacrament, and their union is consummated in the sexual embrace.

To confer this sacrament upon one another, each spouse must freely and publicly consent to the essential requirements of marriage. These essentials are unconditional fidelity, permanence, and openness to life. The priest or deacon will

St. Zelie Martin, in a love letter to her husband, St. Louis Martin, wrote:

"I am longing to be near you, my dear Louis. I love you with all my heart, and I feel my affection so much more when you're not here with me. It would be impossible for me to live apart from you."

ask the couple a series of questions to confirm their intent and consent. The rite of marriage reads: "Have you come here freely, without reservation, to give yourselves to each other in marriage for the rest of your lives? Will you accept children lovingly from God, and raise them according to the law of Christ and his Church?"

This exchange of vows between husband and wife is completed in the sexual exchange of their bodies. Again, we see the sacramental model of the body making visible what is invisible. As a language of the body, sexual intimacy expresses physically the free, total, faithful, and fruitful love that the spouses have vowed to each other.

A "domestic church"

Although only two participate in a marriage, this sacrament has a far-reaching and direct impact upon the whole Church. Marriage creates a "domestic church," which is one reason Catholic weddings take place inside a church building. The married couple will be the first to teach their children about God, the first to form their children in virtue, and the first to set a model for sacrificial love that will leave a lifelong impression. Married spouses bring what happens at the altar into their homes, making home and family the primary place of Christian mission.

> # The love of husband and wife is the force that welds *society* together.
>
> St. John Chrysostom

When we look back into human history, marriage is really the first of all the sacraments. All the others spring from the grace of marriage. As the origin of the family, marriage is the sanctuary of the human person and the building block of civilization.

DISCUSSION QUESTIONS

1. What married couple has really modeled self-gift to you? What do you admire about their marriage and service to each other?

2. How does understanding marriage as a source of sanctifying grace affect how you see marriage?

As the *family* goes ... so goes the whole world.

St. John Paul II

I have found you, and I intend to give myself totally in order to form a truly Christian family.

- St. Gianna Molla,
in a love letter to her then-fiancé, Pietro Molla

Tips

- Many people are surprised to discover that many saints were married. Read about the marriages of holy spouses to find refreshing and quite relatable insight about the marriage vocation. You may find that you and the saints share a lot of the same frustrations and challenges!

- Many parishes and dioceses offer marriage-support activities like couples' retreats, Supper and Substance programs, natural family planning classes, and presentations by dynamic speakers. Check your parish or others in your area for possible events.

- The main goal of marriage is to help others get to heaven. You and your spouse can help each other be accountable to prayer, weekly Mass, and regular confession. Doing these together can also be a powerful way of drawing closer.

Let us go forward in peace, our eyes upon heaven, the only one goal of our labors.

St. Thérèse of Lisieux

Chapter Fourteen

LIVING THE
SEVEN SACRAMENTS

If our minds are open to the power of the sacraments, the next step is to walk in that power. Have you been baptized? Were you confirmed? Are you married? All that was said about the sacraments, all of the grace and transformation that they bring, is all yours. Instead of leaving the serious practice of faith to priests, religious, and "holy people," what if the whole people of God walked in the power of the sacraments? How can we do that?

For starters, receive the sacraments! Go to confession ... today, if possible! Take advantage of the transformative power. Go to Mass and receive communion regularly. Then bring the fruit of that communion home with you. Take it to work with you. Live it in your daily habits and inner life.

With the power of Jesus, break down the walls that separate the sacramental life from your daily life. The key to this is personal prayer, family and friends with whom you can share the sacramental life, and old-fashioned discipline.

In the sacraments, we encounter Christ. Through the sacraments, we come to know Christ is Priest, Bridegroom, and Healer. We are empowered by the Holy Spirit as Jesus promised. And all of this is possible because we are made sons and daughters of our heavenly Father.

You learn to speak by speaking, to study by studying, to run by running, to work by working; and just so, you learn to love by loving. All those who think to learn in any other way deceive themselves.

St. Francis de Sales

Our hope is that this program will help you to walk in closer intimacy with Christ every day. Whether you are a convinced and devout Catholic seeking to deepen your love of the sacraments, a Catholic on the fence looking for answers, or even a non-Catholic trying to understand Catholic sacramental practice, our hope is that this has been about more than information. The aim of the sacraments and all teaching about them is intimacy with Jesus Christ. He is the one who instituted the sacraments so that he could fulfill his promise, "I am with you always, to the close of the age" (Matthew 28:20). If it is Jesus you seek, look no farther than the sacraments of the Catholic Church.

Love God, serve God; everything is in that.

St. Clare of Assisi

DISCUSSION QUESTIONS

1. How has this study affected the way you look at the sacraments? What will you change in your life as a result?

2. Make a list of three ways that you can grow in the power of sacramental life.

3. Who in your life do you need to talk to about finding Jesus in the sacraments?

We are to love God for himself, because of a twofold reason; nothing is more reasonable, nothing more *profitable.*

St. Bernard of Clairvaux

"

Christ said, 'I am the Truth'; he did not say 'I am the custom.'

- St. Toribio

"

Christ be with me, Christ within me, Christ behind me, Christ before me, Christ beside me, Christ to win me, Christ to comfort me and restore me, Christ beneath me, Christ above me, Christ in quiet, Christ in danger, Christ in hearts of all that love me, Christ in mouth of friend and stranger.

- St. Patrick

Tips

- Has this been helpful to you? Recommend this study to a friend.

- Commit to three specific ways to live a life rooted in sacramental grace.

Accept nothing as truth which lacks love. Accept nothing as love that *lacks truth*.

St. Edith Stein

Launch Teens into a Lifelong
Love for the Mass

Altaration: The Mystery of the Mass Revealed by Mark Hart

Altaration addresses head-on one of the biggest problems we all face: how do we get Catholic teens to appreciate the awesome beauty and mystery of the Mass ... and to actually look forward to attending and participating? Featuring some of the very best Catholic speakers, stunning cinematography, and dynamic and engaging workbook materials, *Altaration* meets teens where they are and speaks to their hearts and minds in a language they can understand. Not only will they be taken on a comprehensive and surprising walk through the richness of the Mass, they will also be invited into the throne room ... and into the very heart of God.

5 sessions; includes videos, student workbook, and leader's guide

A **Completely Online Series** that Will Build Communities and Strengthen Your Faith

Featuring Michael Gormley,
co-host of **Catching Foxes** *podcast*

Following Jesus can be difficult, especially in today's world, and it is especially difficult in isolation. For many years, author and speaker Michael Gormley has been helping people come together, form groups, and grow in friendship with each other and Christ. **Don't Walk Alone** is the first in a series of programs designed specifically to build Christ-centered friendships and groups. Get two or three people together, download the free videos and discussion questions, and start having meaningful conversations—together.

Learn How to Make Prayer an Integral Part of **Your Daily Life**

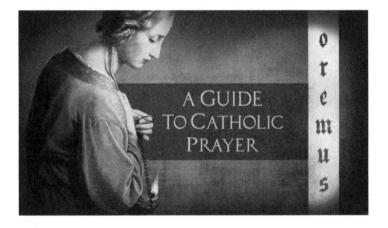

Oremus: A Guide to Catholic Prayer by Fr. Mark Toups

We all desire an intimate relationship with God. But, since learning to "say our prayers" as children, many of us never moved beyond rote recitation to an authentic conversation with God. Prayer can become a source of frustration as we struggle to calm our minds and set aside time to pray. **Oremus,** led by Fr. Mark Toups, teaches the essentials of an effective and fruitful prayer life. Over the course of eight weeks, discover how God speaks to you, even in the smallest encounters.